How to design a
Light

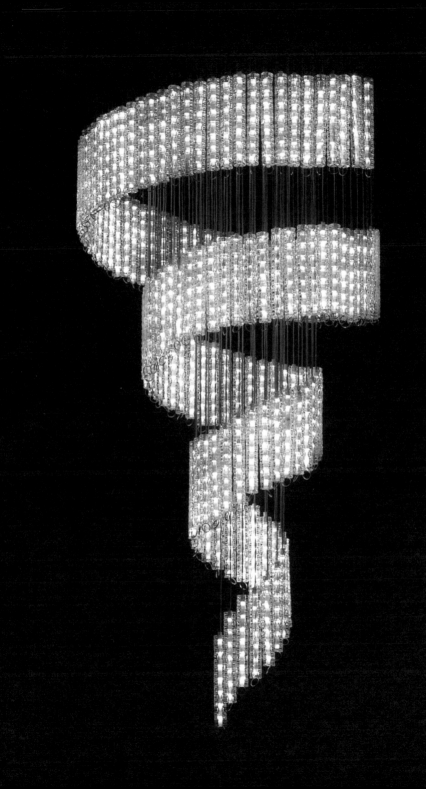

**DESIGN
MUSEUM**

How to design a
Light

conran
OCTOPUS

Previous page:
Ron Arad's Lolita chandelier
(2004) for Swarovksi consists
of a spiralling pixel board that
mixes crystals with LEDs.
The light is interactive: the
pixel board is capable of
displaying text messages
sent via SMS. The name
comes from the opening
of Nabokov's iconic novel:
'Lolita, light of my life…'

How to design a Light

6	Introduction
10	Principles
42	Process
70	Case study: Hakkasan
	Designer: Arnold Chan
108	Index
110	Glossary
111	Picture credits

Introduction

A light is a physical object, just as a chair is a physical object, the specifics of its design shaped variously by aesthetics, technology, materials, engineering and function. But a light is not simply a three-dimensional form: it both occupies space and exists as a means of revealing and describing space. A light *makes* light, and light is a presence that can't be touched, although it is profoundly felt in an emotional sense.

Designing a light inevitably involves designing *with* light. A recessed spotlight that focuses an intense and narrow beam in a particular direction is doing a very different job from a crystal chandelier, whose many-faceted glass drops and ropes of beads, each reflecting individual points of light, create a shimmering, glittering centrepiece. A spotlight is defined purely by its function and is designed either to be concealed or to be paid minimal attention. The focus of attention is that at which the light is directed. In the case of the chandelier, the decorative, theatrical nature of the form is part and parcel of the total effect.

However sleek, quirky, sculptural or otherwise eye-catching a light may be (or however reticent) the quality of the light it emits – its spread, diffusion, direction and colour – is inherently part of the design. A chair implies the act of sitting; a house suggests occupation. A light truly becomes a light only when you turn it on.

Right: A contemporary take on the 'ready-made', the Milk Bottle lamp (1991) by Tejo Remy (1960–) for the Dutch design collective Droog Design puts a bulb into an ordinary milk bottle.

Below: Many lighting schemes for offices rely heavily on long-lasting and economical light sources. Recessed spotlights and concealed light sources mean that the focus is on ambient light, not individual light fittings.

Top right: In the lighting of art galleries or museums, tightly focused spotlights are used to pick out objects. The ambient lighting level is often kept low in order to avoid damage to delicate artefacts such as sculptures and manuscripts.

Below right: A combination of strong natural light and directional spotlights makes an ideal combination for viewing works of art in the Art Institute of Chicago. White walls provide a reflective plane to bounce available light around.

Principles

At the Milan Salone 2009, the Italian lighting manufacturer Flos presented two new lighting designs by Philippe Starck (1949–). Haaa!!! and Hooo!!! (floor lamp and table lamp respectively) both feature crystal elements handmade by Baccarat. Running through the centre of each is a white LED matrix (with electronics designed by Moritz Waldemeyer (1974–) displaying the 'truisms' of American conceptual artist Jenny Holzer: a fivefold collaboration of producer, designers and artist. The invitation to the dinner at which the limited-edition designs were launched consisted of a mirrored cube featuring a tiny LED display that scrolled the text of the invitation, itself the product of considerable research and development. Haaa!!!, which will be made in an edition of nine, costs 90,000 euros; Hooo!!!, which will be made in an edition of 50, costs 9,000 euros.

The conspicuous bling of Haaa!!! and Hooo!!!, along with their hefty price tags and multiple exclamation marks, is in striking contrast to one of Starck's earlier lighting designs (also produced by Flos), the diminutive and appealing Miss Sissi (1991), which has sold in its thousands. With a body, diffuser and support made of injection-moulded coloured polycarbonate, Miss Sissi is an elegant and affordable reworking of the classic café table light. A 'stitched' detail on the shade suggests fabric, a ripple in the base holds the cord neatly in place, and the use of colour gives it a playful quality while accentuating its material homogeneity.

These two projects by the same designer illustrate very different approaches to the principles of lighting design. While Haaa!!! and Hooo!!! make claims for the light as a limited edition artwork, Miss Sissi is self-evidently an industrial product.

Philippe Starck's iconic Miss Sissi light (1991), a reworking of the traditional café table lamp, consists of a body, diffuser and support made of injection-moulded polycarbonate.

Haaa!!! (2009), produced
in a limited edition of nine, is
the result of a collaboration
between designer Philippe
Starck, electronics designer
Moritz Waldemeyer,
producer Flos, the glassware
company Baccarat, which
handmade the crystal
elements, and American
conceptual artist Jenny
Holzer. The text displayed
in the stem of the light
displays Holzer's 'truisms'.

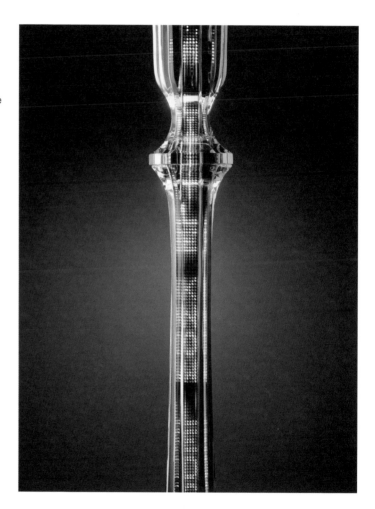

Above left: Mira 50, from UK company John Cullen Lighting, is a fully recessed downlight with a deep black baffle to reduce glare. The beam can be either elongated or spread for a wallwashing effect.

Left: Berenice (1986) by Alberto Meda (1945–), co-designed with Paolo Rizzatto, is a contemporary reworking of the traditional library lamp. Its minimal use of materials reflects the designer's engineering background. The long, articulated arm is made in die-cast aluminium.

Function

The function of a light – or lighting – would appear to be self-evident: to act as a replacement for, or a supplement to, natural light. Its purpose is to enable us to perform routine tasks comfortably when it's dark or gloomy outside, to orientate ourselves in space, and to allow us to navigate safely from place to place so we don't bump into the furniture.

This bottom-line practicality is often further elaborated by breaking function down into distinct categories: background or 'ambient' illumination that gives you light to live by; 'task' lighting, which provides a concentrated, directional boost for work that requires closer concentration; and accent lighting, to pick out points of interest. At the most basic level, designing a light means asking how it will be used. If it is to provide background light, will it be diffused or shaded, or will it target the reflective planes of walls, ceilings and floors? If it is to provide task lighting, to what degree can the light be focused, angled or directed?

For a designer, paying attention to function and practicality also means addressing a host of technical issues: how power is delivered, how the heat of the light source is dissipated, how light levels are controlled by the mechanics of switching and dimming or the electronics of programming; as well as how the light is supported, suspended or articulated, depending on whether a design is free-standing, pendant or adjustable. Whereas a chair must be strong and stable enough to sit on without breaking, but isn't otherwise, or ordinarily, a potentially lethal object, a light, like any other powered appliance or fitting, must meet prescribed safety standards to prevent the risk of fire or electric shock. These are all the more stringent where a light is intended for public or outdoor use, or where, as is the case in bathrooms and showers, it will be used in close proximity to water.

Of all the technical challenges facing designers of lights and lighting designers today, how to incorporate new energy-efficient

15

light sources is among the most pressing. While it is the task of manufacturers to develop sources that are powerful enough and warm enough in colour values to appeal to a domestic market accustomed to incandescent bulbs, it is the designer's role to find a new visual language for these emerging technologies.

El.E.Dee (2001) by the renowned German designer Ingo Maurer (1932–) is a minimal and elegant reinterpretation of an adjustable light. A small circuit board mounted with 204 LEDs is supported by a wand-like stem attached to the base with a ball-and-socket joint that enables the lamp to be tilted and swivelled in any direction. The technology isn't simply bolted on; it informs the entire design.

Below left: Ingo Maurer's El.E.Dee light (2001) reinterprets the task or functional light in terms of new technology, with the design based around the form of the LED circuit board.

Below: Glo-ball (1998) by British designer Jasper Morrison (1959–) uses an etched glass globe to produce gentle ambient light. The light is available in four versions: pendant, two table- or floor-standing lights, and standard lamp.

Diffusion

'I can't stand a naked light bulb, any more than I can a rude remark or a vulgar action,' says the character Blanche DuBois in Tennessee Williams's *A Streetcar Named Desire* (1947). A guiding principle of lighting design is that you should see light, not lights. More specifically, you should not see the light source, or bulb, merely its effect diffused through a shade or reflected from the planes of walls, floors and ceilings. This is to avoid the cardinal sin of lighting design, which is glare.

Glare happens when there is too great a contrast between a light source and its surroundings. Because our eyes have to continually adjust between an over-bright light source and a background that is too dimly lit, we find glare physically tiring and hence emotionally uncomfortable – even stressful, aggressive or intimidating. The bare bulb in the interrogation cell or the spotlight angled to shine directly in the face of the accused are cases in point.

Lighting designers have approached the issue of diffusion in a variety of ways, from the technical or analytic to the poetic. The Akari series of lights, produced by the Japanese American sculptor and designer Isamu Noguchi (1904–88), takes a deceptively simple route. The inspiration for the first Akari designs came about when Noguchi was visiting Japan in the early 1950s and came across a group of night fishermen on the Nagara River in Gifu City.

The fishermen were working by the light of paper lanterns, or *cochin*, which were produced in the area. For Noguchi, the lanterns bobbing over the water evoked a powerful sense of dematerialization. Like the fishermen's *cochin*, his Akari lights are handmade in the traditional way from *washi*, or mulberry bark paper, glued over a springy spiral skeleton of bamboo and mounted on fine metal armatures. Often, and poorly, imitated, Noguchi's paper lanterns make use of the principle of diffusion to create lit sculptures where light appears to float unanchored and adrift in space.

17

The Danish architect, furniture and lighting designer Poul Henningsen (1894–1967) was preoccupied with lighting during the early years of his career. His particular concern was how to achieve with electric sources the same soft, warm quality of light that he remembered from the gaslit interiors of his youth. An intensive period of research into different materials, light diffusion, angles of reflection and colour rendering resulted in the PH series of table and hanging lights, which date from the early 1920s and which have been in production, with a number of modifications, ever since. The lights are composed of separate shades or leaves in overlapping planes to diffuse light and reduce glare. Equally sculptural is the PH Artichoke light (1958), originally created for a Copenhagen restaurant (see page 20). This design consists of 72 separate metal leaves arranged in 12 staggered, descending circular rows so that it is impossible to see the light source from any direction.

Diffusion is given an added dimension when it is the means of creating pattern. Simple pierced or woven shades, or those composed of tiered bands, set up intriguing plays of light and shadow. Garland (2002) by the London-based Dutch designer Tord Boontje (1968–), a mass-market version of his Wednesday light (2002) produced for the retailer Habitat, consists of a delicate filigree of pre-cut metal pressed out of a sheet. When draped around a bulb, this dapples walls and ceilings with soft leaf and petal shapes.

Top right: The Japanese-American sculptor and designer Isamu Noguchi with an Akari mould, Gifu, Japan, 1978.

Below: The Akari series of paper lights create a soft diffusing glow. Inspired by traditional lanterns used by night fishermen, the designs are handmade using mulberry bark paper glued over a bamboo frame. The models shown here are: 3X, 4N, 2N, 5X and 1P.

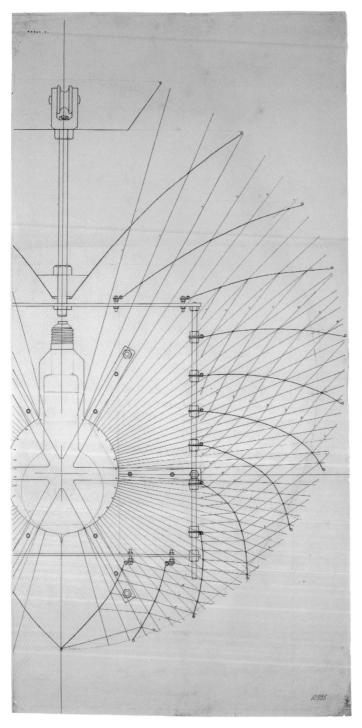

Left: Poul Henningsen's drawing of the 12-shade one-metre-diameter PH Artichoke light (1958) he designed for the Danish National Pavilion. The main angles of light from the bulb formed the basis for the construction. The zigzagging lines connect the points on each shade where the light shines in the same direction. On the basis of this analysis, Henningsen was able to experiment with the outer shape of the lamp without having to make a new drawing each time.

Right: The Langelinie Pavilion, Copenhagen, in 1959, showing Henningsen's PH Artichoke light in situ.

Left: Tord Boontje's Wednesday light (2002) was the limited-edition forerunner of the mass-market Garland light he produced the same year for Habitat. A strand of leaf and floral shapes made of reflective metal is draped around a light bulb to create a dappled effect, with the user determining the form.

Right: Ingo Mauer's Zettel'z 6 light (1998) also invites participation. The light comes ready for assembly, with various sheets of Japanese notepaper clipped onto stainless steel wire cables determining the form and level of diffusion. Thirty-one of the sheets are printed with notes and 49 are blank for customization. One of the ready-printed notes reads: 'These lamps need a co-designer with fantasy and patience. I. M.'

Fig. 4.

Fig. 5.

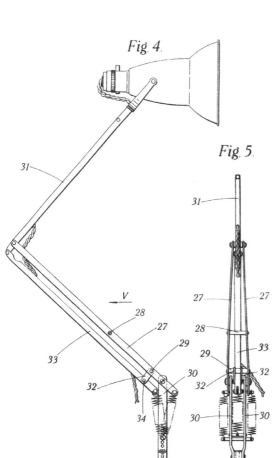

31

V

28

27

33

29

32

30

34

31

27   27

28

33

29

32

32

30   30

24

Above left: 1930s promotional
poster designed by Herbert
Terry & Sons Limited for the
1227 Anglepoise lamp.

Left: 1935 Canadian patent
drawing for the 1227
Anglepoise lamp, designed
by British automotive
engineer George Carwardine.

Direction

Directional light generally implies some form of articulation, so that light can be angled or targeted at a horizontal or vertical surface. Uplights, downlights, eyeball spots that swivel, wallwashers, rise-and-fall pendants and other movable fittings are all forms of directional light, even if the result amounts to a form of diffusion.

The first-ever adjustable free-standing task light was the Anglepoise, designed by British automotive engineer George Carwardine (1887–1947) in 1932. Carwardine, who specialized in vehicle suspension systems, saw the potential of using springs to provide the flexibility and tension necessary to allow a light to be easily adjusted, and once adjusted to remain in the same position. With its jointed metal rods and springs anchored to a heavy base, the articulation of the lamp recalls the anatomy of human limbs. Happily, Carwardine's newly patented design was taken up by the British firm Herbert Terry & Sons, who had at that time been looking for a wider market to promote their springs. The Anglepoise, or versions of it, have been in continuous production ever since.

If the Anglepoise is an archetype, the Tizio task light (1972), designed by German industrial designer Richard Sapper (1932–), has attained the status of a design icon. A precise balancing mechanism allows the light to be repositioned at the touch of a finger. Low-voltage power routed directly through the metal armature avoids trailing cables and preserves the minimal quality of the design, with its instantly recognizable graphic silhouette.

Tolomeo (1987) by the Italian designers Michele De Lucchi (1951–) and Giancarlo Fassina (1935–) is a classic of contemporary Italian lighting design. This updated version of the articulated task light has a small shade shaped like a basin, with a hole pierced in the rear, supported by a jointed, tensile framework. A small protruding handle on the rim of the shade allows you to reposition the light without burning your fingers.

26

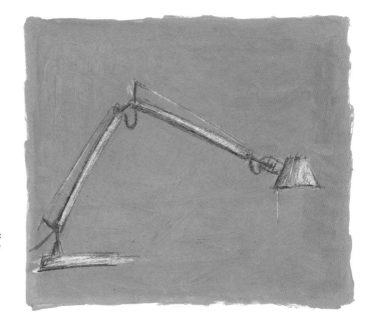

Left: Richard Sapper's Tizio task light (1972) features a precise balancing mechanism that allows the light to be repositioned at the touch of a finger. The graphic silhouette is uninterrupted by cabling; instead, low-voltage power is routed directly through the metal armature.

Right and below: Drawings for the Tolomeo light (1987) by Michele de Lucchi and Giancarlo Fassina.

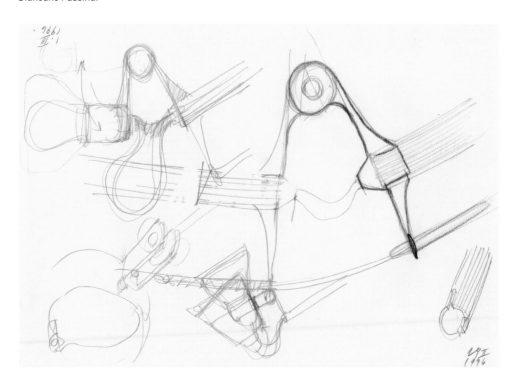

Spatial description

'Furniture, style, carpets, everything in the home is unimportant compared to the positioning of the lighting. It doesn't cost money to light a room correctly, but it does require culture,' wrote the Danish designer Poul Henningsen.

Light describes space and determines to a large extent whether we find a particular environment welcoming or threatening, enclosing or lofty, intriguing or banal. Light a ceiling and you raise the roof; light the walls and you push back the boundaries. Position individual lights around a room at different heights, or delineate pathways at low level, and you invite exploration.

Another type of spatial description occurs when lighting is used to accentuate form or to bring out textural contrast and material character. Here it is light's partner, shadow, that is doing the work. Graze light across painted brickwork and you reveal the tactile qualities of the surface where shadows fall in the dips, hollows and ridges. Sidelight a vase and you emphasize its contours.

When architects design with light, they often conceal it within the structure or furniture of a space – in recesses, in coves, or above and below fitted elements. Backlit panels fronting fixtures such as bathtubs or storage units are other instances where light-as-object is effaced to leave simply its effect or presence. It is perfectly possible to light a space atmospherically and functionally without any light fittings being visible at all.

Yet while there is no practical need for light-as-object, it has never gone away, and over the years basic types of light – pendant light, floor lamp, table lamp – have been continually reinterpreted. The spatial marker of the free-standing floor light, with its strong vertical emphasis, is a form to which lighting designers have returned again and again. Pietro Chiesa's (1892–1948) Luminator (1933), reissued by Fontana Arte, is as futuristic as anyone would wish, with its conical metal reflector and integral stem. The Jill light

Right: Verner Panton's (1926–98) Shell lights (1964) in a 'fun' dining room at a private residence. These designs do not so much describe space as create it, their forms suggestive of stalactites.

Below: Max Ingrand's Fontana table lamp (1954) features a base and shade made of white blown glass. Base, shade or rim can be lit individually or in different combinations.

Left: The standard lamp is a classic light fitting and one that has been reinterpreted over the years. Philippe Starck's Romeo Moon (1998), one of a range that also includes hanging lights, has a reeded clear glass diffuser, steel stem and die-cast aluminium base.

Below: Tom Dixon's playful Jack light (1996) explores the notion of light-as-object.

(1978), designed by the Milan-based duo Perry King and Santiago Miranda, was an iconic design of the late 1970s and early 1980s and one of the first lights to exploit the potential of bright-white tungsten halogen. With its flared angled support, the Montjuic (1990) uplight, by Valencian architect and sculptor Santiago Calatrava (1951–), reveals its designer's engineering preoccupations, as well as his interest in natural organic forms.

Further exploration of the light-as-object can be seen in Fontana (1954), designed by Max Ingrand (1908–69), a noted French stained-glass artist and designer. Fontana offers an evocative interplay of form and filtered light. A distillation of the classic table lamp in appearance, with base and shade made of white blown glass, the design features concealed bulbs so that base, shade or rim can be lit individually or together. An over-scaled star-shaped jack made of polypropylene, Jack (1996), by the British designer Tom Dixon (1959–), is a light, a stackable seat and a sculptural form with a humorous twist, all rolled into one.

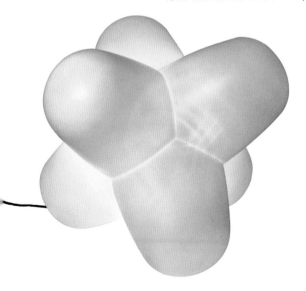

Emotion

Light is profoundly celebratory. From the candles on a birthday cake to the firework display, the decorative traditions of Christmas, Hanukkah and Divali, light plays a central role in festivities around the world. On such occasions, it is the ability of light to create a spectacle that stirs emotion and taps into the collective unconscious.

With advances in technology, such performances can become ever more awe-inspiring and evocative. In 2008 the London-based design collective UVA (United Visual Artists) was commissioned to create a Christmas light installation for the market halls of Covent Garden. *Constellation* consisted of 600 custom-designed mirrored LED tubes hung over the main space, accentuating the volume enclosed by the barrel-vaulted roof. Points and lines of light travelling along the tubes and changing colour created a three-dimensional light show, controllable by an interactive custom-designed panel.

Ingo Maurer has consistently achieved a high degree of technical perfection, and was among the first to explore new light sources such as LEDs. However, a craft or handmade element has remained crucial in his work. One of his particular concerns is to avoid a slick or over-analytical approach, and to embrace the potential of chance and emotion in the design process. 'Emotion is behind each of my lamps,' he has said.

Nothing illustrates this more vividly than Porca Misèria (1994). (The name, which roughly translates from the Italian as 'Life's a bitch!', was derived from the initial responses to the light when it was first exhibited at Milan.) This exploded form is a freeze-framed domestic dispute – the smashed crockery and flying knives, forks and spoons creating a furious kinetic display. You can almost hear the shouting and cries of dismay – an accident or tantrum that is frozen in time. The process of creating the piece builds chance into the result. Each light takes four people almost five days to produce.

Right: British artist Ron Haselden (1944–) works in light, sound, film and video. His *Echelle* ('Ladder'), a neon lightwork, was originally commissioned by the Salisbury Festival in 1999 and formed part of Lumière, a festival of light produced by Artichoke in Durham, 2009.

Left: Lacrime del Pescatore ('The Fisherman's Tears') designed by Ingo Maurer in 2009 evokes the sight of dewdrops glittering on fishermen's nets. It consists of layered nylon nets in three sizes to which are attached 350 crystals. The actual light source, a halogen bulb, is separate and is mounted to the wall.

Right: One of Maurer's best-known designs is Lucellino (1992), a light bulb with goose-feather wings. This is the wall-mounted version.

Left: Porca Miseria (1994) by Ingo Maurer takes the form of an assemblage of smashed crockery and flying knives, forks and spoons. The name roughly translates from the Italian as 'Life's a bitch!'

Below: *Constellation*, a Christmas light installation created in 2008 by the London-based design collective UVA (United Visual Artists) for Covent Garden market. Six hundred mirrored LED tubes, hung over the main space and controlled by an interactive panel, provided a light show of changing colours.

Ordinary porcelain plates are bought in from a supplier, then hammered or smashed on the floor, with the design element consisting of selecting and assembling different sizes and shapes of fragments from the wreckage.

Emotion of a gentler kind imbues Maurer's Lacrime del Pescatore ('The Fisherman's Tears' 2009) – a poetic evocation of dewdrops that the designer saw glittering on fishing nets in Venice. Maurer grew up on an island in Lake Constance, and traces an early source of inspiration to the way the light played on the water.

Colour

When colour is paired with light, various emotional associations naturally come into play. Yet in a domestic setting, where artificial light is intended as an approximation of daylight, we can also be affected subliminally by the tone of different light sources and by the way they render colour. No one could dispute that the incandescent bulb, which turns 95 per cent of the energy it consumes into heat rather than light, and which has a very short lifespan, is inherently wasteful as a light source. What we like about it and find hard to forego is its exceptionally forgiving colour temperature. Compared to the absolute standard of daylight, the incandescent bulb is warm and yellow in tone, flattering for the human complexion, intimate and close to candlelight. In comparison, standard fluorescent light has a greenish cast, which we find much less hospitable and which makes us not only look pasty but also feel edgy and ill at ease.

Fluorescent light has a development history that goes back as far as incandescent sources. In the late nineteenth century Thomas Edison (1847–1931), after reviewing contemporary research, briefly considered its commercial potential, and one of his former employees, Daniel McFarlan Moore (1869–1936), developed the technology sufficiently to see its introduction into stores and offices in the early twentieth century. Many refinements, patents and disputes later, fluorescent lamps were introduced to the market in four different sizes in 1938 by the US firm General Electric, and were showcased at the New York World's Fair the following year. After the outbreak of the World War II, when military and industrial manufacture dramatically increased, demand grew exponentially for this cheap and long-lasting light source, and by the early 1950s the use of fluorescent light in factories, schools and offices meant that its application far exceeded that of incandescent light in the United States. In the home, however, fluorescent lighting was largely relegated to the garage, shed, utility room and other workaday locations.

Right: Fluorescent light sources have improved in recent years, but still tend to have a greenish cast in comparison with halogen and tungsten sources. Their great advantage, aside from the fact that they are relatively long-lasting and energy-efficient, is that they do not emit much heat, which means they can be used in close proximity to other materials without the risk of fire. Here fluorescent strip lights have been used to backlight a splashback.

Below: New compact fluorescents (CFLs) come in various forms, such as this coiled lamp.

Left and below: Tungsten light sources, familiar to us since the days of Edison, typically produce a warm, flattering light. These bulbs convert 95 per cent of the energy they consume into heat, and are due to be phased out in many countries in the coming years.

Bottom and below right: Halogen emits a bright white light that is much closer to daylight and better at colour rendering. It is ideal in any situation where precise colour judgements need to be made. In a contemporary kitchen, it lends crispness to reflective surfaces.

The perceived colour of light from a given source is one thing; colour rendering is quite another. Halogen, which migrated from commercial and retail applications into the domestic sector during the 1980s, emits a true white light, ideal for displaying accurate colour values. The development of low-voltage halogen, along with small and lightweight electronic transformers, vastly extended the application of halogen lighting in domestic settings.

A soft, warm, energy-efficient source of sufficient power and brightness is tantalizingly within reach. Most lighting designers expect that this will soon be achieved with LEDs, rather than the low-energy sources of CFLs (compact fluorescents), despite recent improvements in the quality of the light these emit.

Process

For most people, 'artificial' lighting is synonymous with electric light. Yet for millennia before the first incandescent bulb, shelters, dwellings and buildings of various descriptions were illuminated by a variety of what can only be called, in comparison to daylight, artificial means: firelight, rush lights, candles made of tallow or beeswax, oil lamps and gasoliers. Along the way, people discovered how to amplify such sources through the reflection of shiny or mirrored surfaces.

Candles – particularly those made of beeswax, which gave a better quality of light, and did not splutter or give off a rancid smell like those made of tallow or rendered animal fat – were a relatively expensive item in a household budget. Their cost, along with the low levels of light they produced, meant that the majority of the ordinary working population oriented their lives by daylight, rising at dawn and going to bed when night fell.

In less than a century and a half, electric light has changed the way we live out of all recognition and made the experience of darkness optional for many of us. Today, with the familiar incandescent light bulb on the way out and new technologies such as LEDs and light-emitting materials on the brink of mainstream use, a further dramatic shift is underway.

Above right: For centuries, 'artificial' light meant firelight and candles in their various forms.

Below right: The Lantern Parade at the Midwinter Carnival, Dunedin, South Island, New Zealand.

43

The electric age

The American inventor Thomas Edison is widely credited with the
invention of the incandescent light bulb, which he patented in 1879.
In fact, Edison was not the first to come up with the idea or even
the first to patent it, but he was responsible for making the light
bulb a practical, desirable product and thereby creating a demand
for electricity itself.

The first house in New York City to be lit electrically was the
mansion of millionaire financier John Pierpont Morgan in 1883,
where the new technology was proudly displayed in the form of
bare light bulbs hung round the perimeter of the ornate Pompeiian-
style drawing room. By the early decades of the twentieth century,
electric light was becoming an established amenity in more
ordinary homes.

Very early on, it became apparent that the problem of glare needed
to be addressed. Even at the low wattages of those early bulbs,
light levels were still much higher than they had been in the days of
candlelight and gaslight. All of a sudden what had been shrouded
in mystery, privacy and intimacy was in plain, dazzling view. Not
everyone thought this was a change for the better, and attempts
were soon made to dim the brightness of electric light by shading it.

Just as the design of early automobiles, or 'horseless carriages',
harked back to the mode of transportation they had superseded,
so early light fittings borrowed the reassuring and suggestive forms
of candlesticks, gas mantles, chandeliers and lanterns. Particularly
popular were pendants and lamps featuring coloured glass
shades, such as those produced by the American firm Tiffany in the
Art Nouveau style. Barely two decades after the electric light was
invented, it was already serving as a vehicle for applied decoration.

Electric light opened up other exciting possibilities. One of the first
to recognize its potential both for the theatre and for photography
was Mariano Fortuny y Madrazo (1871–1949), a Spanish-born

designer and polymath who spent much of his working life in Venice. While Fortuny is better known today for the fine pleated-silk dresses he created that became the height of fashion for artistic women during the 1920s, he was also an early pioneer of stage lighting and the inventor of the dimmer switch. The Fortuny light, patented in 1903 and designed for use on the stage, still looks astonishingly modern today. Mounted on a robust steel tripod, an over-scaled cotton hemisphere diffuses light reflected off a concave metal panel. Much later, with the arrival of hi-tech in the 1970s, similar technical or photographic lights began to be seen in domestic interiors.

Below: When electric light was first introduced into homes, bulbs were often unshaded. This Victorian drawing room features wall fittings with bare bulbs (only one of which is switched on). Plate from *The Electric Light in our Homes* by Robert Hammond, published in London in 1884.

Modernism

'We can have concealed lighting or we can have diffused and projecting lighting... A hundred-candle-power lamp weighs less than two ounces, but there are chandeliers weighing nearly two hundredweight with elaborations in bronze or wood, and so huge that they fill up all the middle of the room; the upkeep of these horrors is a terrible task because of the flies.' Le Corbusier, *Vers une architecture* ('Towards a New Architecture'; 1923)

Electric light was clean. It did not discolour interior surfaces, as gas jets and candles had done, and walls and ceilings no longer needed to be painted in dark colours to obscure the traces of smuts and fumes. In the 1920s the society decorator Syrie Maugham (1879–1955) caused a sensation with her all-white rooms – pristine schemes made possible by the electric age.

While in the average home light fittings were cloaked in acceptably decorative dress, the radical designers and architects of the first wave of modernism in the early decades of the twentieth century approached the design of light fittings in a more mechanistic way. The functional nature of the unadorned electric bulb or tube struck a chord with those intent on a pared-back aesthetic, and whose points of reference included the aeroplane, automobile, grain silo and passenger liner.

Oddly, very few lights were produced by the Bauhaus; the most notable was the WG 24 (1923–4 often known as the *Wagenfeld Lampe*) designed by Wilhelm Wagenfeld (1900–90) in collaboration with fellow Bauhaus student Karl J Jucker (1902–97). First exhibited at the Leipzig Trade Fair in 1924, the table lamp consisted of a milky-white glass shade, similar to those used in factories, mounted on a clear-glass stem and base. Steel tubing inside the stem carried the wiring. At the time the light proved too expensive to produce for the mass market – a common fate of many early modernist designs – but it has since been reissued and is in production today.

Light, with its ability to describe volume, and its association with health and well-being, was a preoccupation of modernist architects. Le Corbusier's (1887–1965) handling of artificial lighting arrangements, however, particularly in his early villas, was less successful than his manipulation of natural light and shade. It was a problem that he himself appreciated. Le Corbusier understood that the best way of treating electric lighting, which could be 'intense' and 'sharp', was to diffuse it in some fashion, through the use of reflectors or fixtures that directed the light upwards to bounce off walls and ceiling planes. 'We blunder with the stammerings of a totally new invention,' he wrote.

Le Corbusier's early 'blunderings' with the lighting arrangements at Villa La Roche (1925), in Paris, caused some consternation. When the building was first handed over, most of the lights were strip lights, mounted on the wall or housed in reflectors. In the gallery, the seven bulbs in the strip light mounted along the bottom of the windows produced so little illumination that his client, Raoul La Roche, complained: 'even when all seven lamps are on, you can barely see to read.' After holes were punched in the dining room ceiling to accommodate a system of ceiling lights, La Roche's patience wore thin:

> I understand perfectly your hesitancy over the way to light my house. But until you find something really good, it is essential at least that I should be able to see clearly in my home. It's six months since I moved in and I am still obliged to use illumination, which, particularly in the painting gallery, relies on ad hoc arrangements. [The 'ad hoc arrangements' consisted of seven bulbs strung on wires to light the gallery.]

Matters were resolved only in 1928, three years after the house was completed, when a trough fitting housing 25 bulbs was installed in the gallery, boosting the illumination considerably.

Around the same time, the Irish pioneering designer Eileen Gray (1878–1976) was working on the design of her own villa at

Right: Wilhelm Wagenfeld's WG24 light (1923–4) was the most notable lighting design to come out of the Bauhaus. The machine aesthetic is expressed in the tubular stem, metal base and globular shade, reminiscent of factory lights. Wagenfeld designed the light in collaboration with a fellow Bauhaus student, artist Karl Jucker (1902–97).

Roquebrune-Cap-Martin in the south of France. Her Tube light (1927) exhibits the same functionalism as early modernist designs, but with the welcome addition of a degree of elegance and finesse. The light takes the form of a simple vertical tube supported by a thin chromium-plated steel frame.

'Industry is the style of the twentieth century, its mode of creation,' Giò Ponti (1891–1979) famously said in 1925. A prolific designer, architect and writer Ponti was the founder of the influential architecture and design magazine *Domus*, as well as of the lighting and furniture company Fontana Arte. His 0024 hanging light (1931) is another modernist classic. A central diffuser made of sandblasted glass conceals the bulb, while surrounding the diffuser are concentric transparent glass discs held in place by a chrome-plated brass frame.

Below left: Eileen Gray's Tube light (1927) reveals a characteristic modernist stance in its avoidance of any decorative embellishment.

Right: Giò Ponti's 0024 hanging light (1931) is still produced today. The central diffuser and concentric discs are made of glass.

Below right: A 1967 drawing by Giò Ponti, showing a variation of the Bilia lamp he designed in 1931 for Fontana Arte, which is still in production.

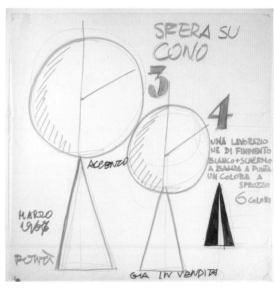

51

Left: With its furled organic form realized in plastic, Vico Magistretti's Chimera light (1969) represented a departure from the strict rationalism of postwar Italian design. The drama of the design is enhanced by its size: the light is six feet tall.

Rationalism and reconstruction

Not even the most casual student of design could fail to appreciate the dominance of Italian designers in the field of lighting in the postwar period. In the aftermath of the World War II, as part of the *ricostruzione*, or reconstruction, of the shattered Italian economy, a creative partnership grew up between architects, designers and manufacturers. It was to result in a unique culture where good design was seen not as elitist but as a fundamental part of the good life, *la dolce vita.* Such a culture also proved eminently marketable and exportable, with design creating added value or a cachet for international consumers. During the 1940s, 1950s, 1960s and beyond, Italian designers put their mark on a whole range of products, from typewriters to furniture, from cars to scooters. 'Our ideal of the good life and a level of taste and thought expressed by our homes and manner of living are all part of the same thing,' wrote Giò Ponti in *Domus* in 1947.

Lighting played an integral role in the enthusiastic reception of Italian design worldwide, and its attendant association with quality and modernity. As industrial products, light fittings do not, by and large, require huge capital investment in the form of plant or tooling. They are also the perfect vehicle for the expression of design thought and technical innovation, both of which came to typify contemporary Italian design. Furthermore, Italian craft traditions, for example in glass-making, provided both an element of continuity and a fruitful base for material experimentation. This is a link that has persisted. In 1981, the lighting company Foscarini was founded in Venice to explore the potential of Murano glass. Among its founder members was Ettore Sottsass (1917–2007), better known as the initiator of the postmodernist Memphis style.

From the outset, a defining feature of contemporary Italian design was rationalism, an Italian version of modernism promoted in the pages of *Domus.* Leading designers included the Castiglioni brothers, Gino Sarfatti, Pietro Chiesa and Vico Magistretti. Producers and manufacturers included Fontana Arte, Flos,

Luceplan, Arteluce and Artemide, which remain leading international brands today. The career of Gino Sarfatti (1912–84) typified the way in which design became an integral part of Italian manufacture in the postwar period. Originally trained as an engineer, Sarfatti began working in the lighting industry in the late 1930s and subsequently set up Arteluce, an important Italian lighting manufacturer that provided a platform for collaborations with many of the leading Italian designers of the 1950s and 1960s. Sarfatti himself was dedicated to research and innovation in far-ranging fields, from light sources to production techniques and materials. Over a period of 30 years, he designed more than 400 lights, some of which made expressive reference to contemporary art and sculpture, such as the mobiles of Alexander Calder. One of Sarfatti's most famous designs is the 2097/50 hanging light (1958), a contemporary version of a chandelier with multiple curving branches supporting 50 frosted lamps arranged in a spiral.

A similar departure from the strict rationalism of the immediate postwar period was Vico Magistretti's (1920-2006) floor lamp Chimera (1969), which reflected the designer's interest in the new plastics technology.

Right: Gino Sarfatti was an incredibly prolific designer. His elegant 2097/50 hanging light (1958) features 50 frosted bulbs supported on curving branches arranged in a spiral.

Ready-mades

Of all the designers associated with the pre-eminence of Italian lighting, the Milanese Castiglioni brothers, Achille (1918–2002) and Pier Giacomo (1913–68) have been among the best known, and most prolific and commercially successful. Sons of a sculptor, the brothers established their own design studio in the 1940s.

Wit is a characteristic of many Castiglioni designs: 'There has to be irony, both in design and in the objects. I see around me a professional disease of taking everything too seriously. One of my secrets is to joke all the time,' Achille has written. Crucial, too, is the influence of the ready-made school of art, typified by Marcel Duchamp's 'found objects'. Their Mezzandro stool (1957), for example, famously incorporated a tractor seat.

Two of the best-known lighting designs that display the ready-made approach are the Toio (1962) and the Parentesi (1970), the

Right: The Arco lamp (1962), a contemporary classic, was designed by Achille and Pier Giacomo Castiglioni. The marble base, which weighs 100 lb, supports a curved aluminium stem from which a polished aluminium shade is suspended.

Below left: Sketch illustrating the components of the Arco.

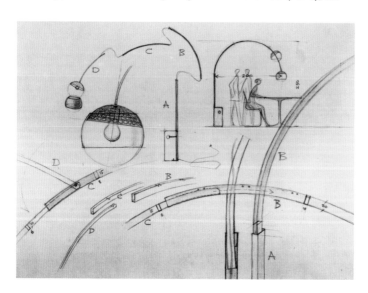

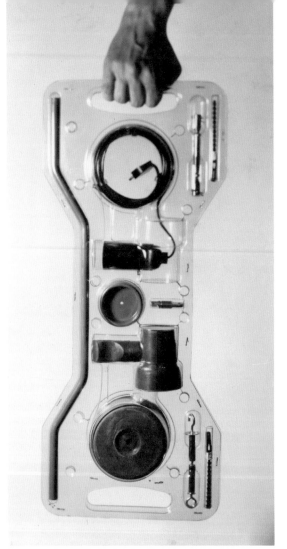

latter the result of a collaboration between Achille and the
renowned Fiat designer Pio Manzù. Toio, with its defiant exposure
of working parts, came about when the brothers were challenged
to design a light from everyday objects that might be found in a
garage. The prototype makes use of a fishing rod for the stand or
support, braced by a band saw, with a halogen car headlamp as
the light source. Parentesi also features a car reflector lamp,
which is attached to a metal sleeve that can be moved up and
down a taut steel cable strung between floor and ceiling.

Perhaps the Castiglionis' most iconic design, however, dates from
1962. The Arco floor lamp reflects the designers' critical approach
and determination to rethink function and translate it into form.
('Start from scratch. Stick to common sense. Know your goals and
means,' Achille advised his students.) The Arco comprises a marble
base, weighing 100 lb, which supports an attenuated aluminium
stem. At the end of this is suspended a pierced hemispherical
aluminium shade. The arc of the stem, which also acts as a channel
for the cable, can be adjusted to different heights. The contrast
between the monumental base and the curve of the springy stem
describes a dynamic spatial volume. In that sense, both the design
of the fitting and the light it emits are doing very similar jobs.

In the 1960s, the ready-made approach to lighting design was
radical. More recently, young designers have returned to the same
conceptual stance, either to shake up our preconceptions or to make
commentaries on our throwaway society. Milk Bottle lamp (1991) by
Tejo Remy (1960–), for the influential Dutch collective Droog Design,
puts a bulb into an ordinary milk bottle. Clothes Hanger lamp (2002),
created by Héctor Serrano (1978–) for the same company, consists
of a low-voltage light suspended from a hanger – you create the
shade yourself by draping the hanger with a piece of clothing.
Eight-Fifty (2001) by Claire Norcross is a table or standing lamp
made from a bristling array of plastic cable ties used in industrial
packaging (or in stainless steel for a limited edition), while Styrene
(2003) by Paul Cocksedge (1978–) is a pendant shade that diffuses
light through an organic form composed of baked polystyrene cups.

Left: The design of the Toio lamp (1962) by Achille and Pier Giacomo Castiglioni came about when the brothers were challenged to come up with a light fitting that could be made out of everyday items that might be found in a garage.

Above right: Paul Cocksedge's Styrene pendant light (2003) diffuses light through an organic form made of baked polystyrene cups, discarded in their millions every day.

Below right: Limited edition of the Eight-Fifty light (2001) by Claire Norcross produced for Ferrious. Stainless steel cable ties attached to a chimney cowl form a bristling diffuser. Norcross, whose degree was in embroidery, used textile and basketry skills to come up with the design. A pendant version was put into production by Habitat the following year.

Left: 85 Lamps (1993) by
the Dutch designer Rody
Graumans (1968–) for Droog
Design takes as its point of
departure only the essentials:
bulbs, wires and connectors.
Multiplying these basic
elements achieves a kind of
opulence: 'less' and 'more'.

Right: The playful Clothes
Hanger lamp (2002) by
Héctor Serrano, also for
Droog, consists of a low-
voltage light suspended
from a hanger.

Track, wire and fibre

A significant development in the late twentieth century was the migration into the everyday domestic interior of light sources and fittings originally designed for use in the retail and commercial sectors. Designers such as the partnership of Franco Bettonica (1927–99) and Mario Melocchi (1931–), responsible for the Tenso system (1998), brought a rigorously architectural aesthetic to track lighting, which was otherwise dominated by workaday mass-market products.

The arrival of low-voltage halogen, which coincided with a trend towards minimalism in interior design, resulted in lighting designs with barely visible means of support. Bare-wire installations featuring tensioned cables along which tiny low-voltage halogen spots were positioned brought an element of museum or retail display into the home. In the Chopstick light by Shui-Kay Kan the halogen spots rest on fine rigid arms spanning the cables.

In fibre optics, light travels the length of coated strands of acrylic or fibreglass, emerging as single points of light. The light source is a light box, which can be located far from the point where the light is actually emitted. This makes fibre optics the ideal solution in situations where delicate material might be damaged by heat or in combination with water – in lighting swimming pools, for example, or running taps and showerheads. Sharon Marston, a British designer with a background in jewellery and costume design, combines woven nylon, polymer fibre optics, monofilament and polypropylene to create lyrical one-off pieces that blur the boundary between light and art installation.

Above right: The Tenso system of track lighting (1998), designed by Franco Bettonica and Mario Melocchi can be used to create a variety of effects. The track can be mounted horizontally, vertically or diagonally.

Below right: The Laelia light by Sharon Marston is formed of delicate leaf shapes suspended from a chromed dome using ultrafine fibre-optic filaments. The filaments are arranged in a meandering pattern that echoes the organic form of the glass shapes.

Left, above and below: *Field of Light* (2008–9), a lighting installation by artist and designer Bruce Munro at the Eden Project in Cornwall. The installation, on the sloping grass roof of the visitors' centre, consisted of 6,000 acrylic stems enclosing fibre-optic cables and crowned with clear glass spheres.

Below: Life 01 (2009) designed by Paul Cocksedge.

Back to the future

Since the digital revolution, we have increasingly entertained ourselves by sitting in front of screens that are light sources in themselves – phones, computers, giant plasma screens. Yet while the developed world is light-polluted, so bright at night that we cannot see the stars, in other parts of the globe there is next to no power infrastructure at all. This disparity, and the looming environmental crisis, will shape the nature of lights to come.

'In Praise of Shadows', a temporary exhibition mounted as part of London Design Festival 2009, featured the work of 21 European designers exploring the potential of low-energy lighting and the evocative nature of darkness. The theme of the exhibition was inspired by the European Union directive to phase out low-efficiency light bulbs by 2012. Life 01 (2009), designed by Paul Cocksedge (1978–) and produced by Flos, consists of a crystal vase part-filled with water and holding a single flower stem. The stem of the flower acts as an electrical conductor and activates a light source of small LEDs in the bottom of the vase. As the flower withers, the light gradually fades and disappears.

Featured in the same exhibition was Sonumbra (2006), by Loop.ph, a design research studio in London experimenting with the potential of light-responsive textiles. Sonumbra, conceived with African villages in mind but first realized as a play space in a Sunderland park, consists of an outsize parasol of light-responsive fabric. During the day the canopy provides shade; during the night it emits light, powered and collected by solar cells embedded in the material.

Left: Sonumbra (2006)
by Loop.ph consists of an
outsize parasol of light-
responsive fabric. During
the day the canopy provides
shade; during the night it
emits light-powered and
collected by the solar cells
embedded in the material.

Case study:
Hakkasan

Designer:
Arnold Chan

Interview with Arnold Chan

Arnold Chan is one of the world's leading lighting designers. After training initially as an architect, he turned to lighting design in the early 1980s, founding Isometrix Lighting + Design in 1985. Since then he has collaborated with some of the world's most renowned architects, including David Chipperfield, John Pawson, Zaha Hadid, Richard Rogers, Philippe Starck and Jean Nouvel. His projects have included the St Martin's Lane Hotel (with Starck, 1999) for the US hotelier Ian Shrager; exterior lighting for the London department store Selfridges; Damian Hirst's fashionable Notting Hill restaurant Pharmacy (1997); and the Gramercy Park Hotel, New York (2007). Emblematic of his playful, innovative approach are the 'rainbow'-coloured headboards at the St Martin's Lane Hotel, where guests are invited to change the lighting to create their own 'mood'.

In 2001, Chan collaborated with the French architect and interior designer Christian Liagre (1943–) to create the Oriental fusion restaurant Hakkasan in London's West End, for the restaurateur Alan Yau. Later, he also worked on another of Yau's projects alongside Liagre: Buddakan, in New York.

I trained at the AA and was one of those who remained in design but didn't stay in architecture. I got into lighting by accident while I was still at college. I was doing private work, freelance work, designing showrooms for a manufacturer of technical lighting, which meant I had to understand how technical lights worked.

At that time mainstream lighting was still fairly straightforward and basic. It was still incandescent lights, PAR lamps, downlights, eyeballs, wallwashers, things like that. I was fascinated by the whole idea of technical lighting, and when I finished at the AA I went on to do a year's course at what was then South Bank Poly. The course was on the technical side of lighting, but we weren't taught lighting design.

The profession of lighting design didn't exist in the UK at that time. It was created, like a lot of specialist disciplines within the construction industry, when technology evolved and architects needed more support. If you look back 25 years, architects did everything, and then quite rapidly the situation changed. Now architects have so many different consultants.

Lighting is curious because it's not just technical; there is what I would call a lot of artistry in it. The emotional side of lighting is very important in spaces, in architecture, in our lives. Daylight plays a huge part in the way we feel. It's all about feeling. When we don't get enough sun we all get depressed.

Is the artistic side what attracted you to lighting, do you think?

Yes, it was totally the emotional, the theatrical side of things. How to create an ambience. You need the technical expertise to fulfil the creative side of things. A lot of architects or designers know the feeling that they want to create, but they rely on us to help them achieve it technically. Quite often I'll explain to clients that in the early stages what we're doing is producing an instrument of light, and then at the end we can play it in different ways. This is particularly true in homes or hospitality environments, where there's the need to create different ambiences at different times of day.

It's taken people a long time to understand the importance of lighting. People still buy a fitting without turning it on.

Lighting is the one thing that's not tangible. With a chair, table, a piece of furniture, a floor-standing light, somebody can look at it and decide whether they like it or not. Whereas lighting design is a leap of faith in a way, and clients have to trust that we can give them something at the end that they might be happy with. It's not something that they can see or touch.

You've been in practice quite a while, haven't you? You've got an enormous body of work.

A long time – twenty-five years. Fortunately we've always been with very talented designers and architects, so we learn a lot. I always see my role as that of a bespoke tailor, and I try to complement what the designer is trying to do. I'm never there to impose myself. I'm there to listen and contribute rather than to lay down the rules. Whether we're working with John Pawson or Philippe Starck or David Chipperfield, the end result is always quite different, and it is very much the architect's or designer's personality that comes out.

I think that a successful design project is one where the designer and the client have a certain chemistry together, where they push the envelope with each other. It's much easier to work with somebody who's good. With a really talented designer, if you explain a problem to them, it's very easy for them to change it. You need to be a diplomat in a lot of cases. Especially at this high end, you're dealing with a lot of fragile egos, so you need to be able to rub them up the right way.

How did you get involved with Hakkasan?

I knew Alan Yau, the founder of the restaurant. Nowadays he's very well known and he's been honoured for his services to the hospitality industry. Many years ago, in the middle of the last recession, he created a very successful noodle bar chain called Wagamama. At that time Alan was a graduate student, and he approached John Pawson to do some concept designs for the first restaurant because he couldn't afford him for the whole job. This was before John was well known. Within two months of the restaurant opening it was already doing thousands of covers. It was unbelievable.

I knew Alan from those early Wagamama days. Because I had worked with Christian Liagre for many years and he was comfortable with what I could do for him, I was able to introduce him to Alan to do this project. Alan is passionate about design. Alan's approach has always been to find a space that is unexpected. It's usually in a back alleyway or it's in a basement and therefore the rent is low. The savings from the rent, he puts into design. For every one of his projects he uses the best materials – the second Wagamama was designed by David Chipperfield – there's no expense spared, even down to the details and equipment in the kitchen. The quality of the ingredients is the same – everything is always very high quality.

When Alan found the space for Hakkasan it was a disused strip joint. I remember going to see it in that little alleyway off the back end of Tottenham Court Road and there were syringes everywhere; it was awful. Now it's all cleaned up, but I remember saying to Alan at the time – are you sure people will come here? We were all proven wrong.

Lighting plays a large part in Hakkasan.

Yes, because it's in the basement. It was a project which I think illustrates the brilliance of Christian as a designer, because he was able to turn a very boring basement space into something quite exciting using these pseudo Chinese screens. The screens themselves make the place feel bigger. The ability to see through the screens into another space always adds to the mystery. And the fact that the lighting is very dramatic and dark makes you feel like you need to explore the place.

After you'd introduced the designer to the client, when did you get involved?

Invariably I get involved as early as possible. There's quite a lot of work that I do at the earliest stages of the project, even before I consider lighting. What are the general principles of making an ambience? What is the appropriate ambience? In this kind of project, you want to make people feel not just comfortable, but as one operator put it: 'I need everybody to feel sexy.' To feel like it's a special occasion and it's not just a routine dinner.

This whole concept of fine Eastern dining is a fairly recent one. It's not just about the food any more. Even up until ten years ago, if you went to a Chinese restaurant in Hong Kong where the food was supposed to be exquisite, the room itself would be lit with fluorescent lights. Ten tables of ten… it would be like a canteen.

And, yes, the food would be good, but there would no atmosphere at all. The idea of candlelit dinners and good service, wine, food, music, the whole experience of dining, is quite a recent thing. With Hakkasan, Alan was looking to create an iconic place. What he and Christian came up with was globally unique. It became the first Chinese restaurant to win a Michelin star – and, you know, with Michelin standards it's not just about the food, it's also about the ambience.

The significance of this restaurant within the industry and particularly in Asia was very profound, and set a real precedent. It also opened at a time when restaurants became big business. It wasn't the family restaurateur any more. Instead, you're talking about a two, three, four, five-million-pound investment. Restaurants now have become quite substantial financial undertakings and therefore the risks involved are huge.

What was your initial approach to lighting Hakkasan?

The most important thing was to make the space not feel like a basement, and to create an element of visual surprise. Technically we knew we needed to light all the walls in some way, and not just the tables.

That's about creating a sense of expansiveness, isn't it?

Yes. It's opening up the space. Naturally the eye tends to look forward. You don't automatically look up and down. That means lighting vertical surfaces is always much more important than lighting horizontal surfaces. By lighting the vertical surfaces you can see through to an end, which is important when subconsciously you're trying to feel secure and you need to be able to locate yourself. Psychologically when you know where you stand – literally – you feel comfortable.

Regulations always dictate that you need certain light levels on horizontal planes, but that's only half the story. Because if you only light horizontal planes and no verticals, you get a headache after a while. You can light a place very dimly and it doesn't feel dim because you've lit vertical surfaces.

It's also better to have a lot of different points of light at low wattages than it is to have fewer points at higher wattages. You can do a lot more with that arrangement. It's very comfortable to be bathed or wrapped in light. It's a very nurturing experience. If light is just coming from above, it's rather boring and doesn't engage with us very well. Whereas if you've got light from below, from the sides, from above, so that you are enveloped in light, it's a comfortable feeling.

Everything. We used cold cathode, fluorescent, incandescent, halogen, all the different types of halogen bulbs, some LEDs, the whole range. You have to keep up with the technology. We're being shown new things all the time. But I'm not a big advocate of using technology for technology's sake. It's like having the latest computer. The moment you have it, there's another one coming out. Sometimes the naked flame is the best light, if you can use it. For the new restaurants we're doing with Alan, we're going to be using LEDs. When we were working on the first Hakkasan, LEDs were still in their infancy. As lighting designers we now have to meet the codes for energy efficiency codes and sustainability.

Quite honestly, the technology hasn't quite caught up yet. There isn't the equipment out there that can create the sort of ambiences we want to create. The energy efficient sources tend to be quite harsh and cold and not powerful enough, but they are improving quite quickly. In a matter of months, as opposed to years, we're going to get the right palette of colours in the light sources we're going to need to use.

Do you think the future will be LEDs?

No question. The challenge right now is two things – power and warmth. They need to perfect whites to get as much warmth as possible. Colour temperature is to do with the warmth of the light source, but the other thing we have to pay great attention to is colour rendering, which is the extent to which a light source reveals the true colours of materials. Generally speaking, a very warm light, say incandescent, is not very good at colour rendering. Halogen is better. A very cool fluorescent light, which is what printers use so they can see every colour in the spectrum, is totally unflattering for the face.

The challenge, for example in retail stores, is twofold. You need to be able to see the true colours and textures of the clothing, which means a light source with high colour rendering, but when you try the clothes on you need a warmer and more flattering light. In restaurant terms, you want a brighter, cooler light for fast food or fast casual places, because you don't want people to stay too long.

How did the design of Hakkasan evolve?

While Christian was developing the scheme, we were involved in work sessions deciding where the light was going to be. For example, if we knew we wanted to highlight the table, was it coming from a spotlight in the ceiling, was it a recessed downlight, a surface-mounted spotlight, or was it something hanging over the table? These were some of the design issues we discussed, both with Christian and then with Alan as well.

I think the most important element in Hakkasan, the feature that's most recognized, is the lit blue wall. Christian had the idea of using blue glass, and I said that it would make a huge difference if we backlit it to make a wall of light.

What did you use to backlight the glass?

We used cold cathode. We had to do mock-ups to get as much light down the wall as possible. You'll never get it totally evenly lit – it will always be brighter at the top and bottom – but we developed special reflectors to punch the light through and light the void in between the wall and the glass. To make the colour more saturated, we painted the wall blue. It's a white light catching a blue background bouncing reflected blue light out through blue glass.

What influenced your decision to have the little pendants over the table?

They create a kind of focus and extra drama on the table. When you're sitting there you are aware that there's something hanging over you, focusing on your dishes, and that adds a certain intensity to the experience.

Was it difficult to get the height of the pendants right?

We had to play around and experiment with different heights.
That can be tricky to get right. When we were working on St
Martin's Lane with Philippe Starck, for example, he wanted to
have bare light bulbs in the restaurant. We tried out eight different
types of light bulb to find the one that was warmest, visually the
most appealing and the most flattering on the skin, and eventually
settled on the original Edison – what we call the 'coiled coil'
filament. They were set very low. After the hotel restaurant opened,
we discovered that when people had had a few drinks they liked
to play ping-pong with them. So we had to raise them higher.

The other feature that I think is quite unique at Hakkasan is that
we use some theatrical projectors to light the wall behind the bar
with a ripple effect.

How do they work?

They're stage fittings, rotating drums with slots in them that create
a horizontal ripple. Architectural lighting, stage lighting, and TV
and film lighting are three very different technologies. Film and
theatre equipment generally doesn't work very well in architecture.
The lamp sources don't last long enough. Stage lighting is about
very intricate, subtle control, and the dynamic is always one-
dimensional. You're always looking at the stage, which means
you can hide the lights very easily. Whereas in architecture you're
walking around, you're feeling the lighting. What we had to do
was adapt the fittings technically so they were maintainable, and
integrate them into the design so that they weren't obvious.

That sense of movement is a bit like water, isn't it?

Exactly. Christian originally wanted to create a live wall of moss
behind the bar. But the environmental health officer put a stop to
that, because moss is deemed to be mould and you can't have
mould in a restaurant. Therefore we had to come up with

something else at the last minute to create a little bit of visual excitement. The whole elevation is very horizontal with these slate tiles, so we used the rippling light to create the effect of subterranean water spilling down the wall.

How did you light the screens?

We used a raking light. The screens are very delicate and don't catch much light, so we used strong, narrow pencil beam spots placed very close to the screens to rake them and give moments of highlights. The rest of the time the screens are in silhouette.

The most important thing is what I call the hierarchy of light. You need to know where to draw people's attention. In the case of a restaurant like Hakkasan, the focus is first of all on the table. You need to read the menu and see what you're eating. Then your attention is on the people or person you're dining with. You need to make the visual appearance of people flattering so they feel comfortable. When they feel relaxed, then there's every chance of them enjoying the whole experience. Then when they look up, they catch glimpses of theatre around them – they can see other people, they can catch another face, they can see little highlights of detail. It's not all in darkness; neither is it flatly lit.

And how do you make people look nice?

Reflected light. None of us look very good when lit directly. Photographers do this all the time, they bounce light to create a softer appearance. The quality of the light, the colour temperature of the light, all this is very important.

I remember years ago doing a project for Damien Hirst's restaurant Pharmacy. There is a blue light in the installation of the Pharmacy and we had to go through six or seven types of blue filter to find one that didn't make people look green. He wanted the coolness of the pharmacy look, but obviously it was a dining experience so you didn't want everybody to look as though they were going be ill.

Did you use filters at Hakkasan?

I use them all the time. Even if you have a hunch about what's the right way of doing something, or which are the right filters to use, until you actually come to do the focusing you can't really tell. Every time it's slightly different. For example, there's ten different amber filters you can use, all with very subtle differences in shade and intensity, and I can say, OK here we'll use a certain sort of amber filter, but when we come to focus, it may need two layers or it may need three layers. You don't know until you actually do it.

It's to do with the chemistry, if you will, of all the materials around you: if they're reflecting the light or not reflecting the light. A John Pawson interior will be generally very white, with very reflective surfaces. At Hakkasan, the surfaces are very dark, so the light reacts completely differently. You can have the same light and it looks and feels completely different.

Do you oversee the installation?

We have to check. In most cases, the quality of installation counts a great deal. Positioning is important. Where we're raking that screen, for example, if the light fitting is 30–40 millimetres too far away, it's not going to rake. Or if it's too close, it rakes too sharply. There's got to be a certain precision. We are constantly battling, fighting our corner, to get the installation done to our requirements. We're the ones responsible for delivering the scheme at the end.

To design something to next to no tolerance takes a lot of effort and coordination. In fact, the more decorative a scheme, the more forgiving it is. With John's work, if the wall isn't plastered perfectly when you light it, all the imperfections show up. Right now we're finishing a job in New York with John, and there's some benches that we've lit underneath to make the floor glow. The limestone floor was supposed to be matt but it's turned out to have a slight sheen to it, so you see all the reflections of the bulbs. To fix that we're having to lens everything.

What sort of fine-tuning did you have to do at Hakkasan?

A lot of adjustment. There's a lot of work done in the focusing. For example, the pendant over the table gave a very defined circle of light, so we had to use diffusers in front of the bulb to soften the glow. For the longer tables we had to use what we call a linear spread lens to stretch the light to cover the rectangular surface, and yet we still had to apply louvres to it so that when you're sitting down you can't see the light and there's no glare. The precision and the finesse are down to the fine-tuning at the end.

Creating the appropriate ambience also requires a very sophisticated programmable dimming system to be able to control each particular light, so we can balance the brightness of the light of the table, of the wall, of the hanging lamps so they become one. It becomes one totality. There's nothing worse than having a light that's too bright. That's annoying.

Once the installation is complete, you have to make sure that the instrument is playing properly. All the circuits, all the dimming, it's like tuning a guitar or a piano. When they do the soft opening of the restaurant you'll be fine-tuning the balance, and then a few weeks into service you may change things around. Nobody really knows at the beginning of a project how the place is actually going to behave. Will it attract more of a drinking crowd or a dining crowd? For drinking, you make it more dramatic. For dining, you play down the drama a bit.

In a restaurant there's a natural progression from 6 p.m. and through to 12 p.m. Those who like to eat at 6–7 p.m. are a different type of people to the ones who want to eat at 10–11 p.m., so the ambience changes quite a bit. There's no point being too dramatic too early on.

*So these adjustments would be pre-programmed into
your settings?*

Yes, the settings change automatically. I will probably change the
scene three times through the night. It's so subtle that people don't
know it, yet the ambience at midnight is completely different from
that at seven. Later, there's much more contrast.

When I've been involved in jobs for Ian Schrager – most recently
the Gramercy Park Hotel in New York – he implicitly trusts the
setting that I create with him. It takes an extraordinary amount of
time – it might take up to six sessions after the hotel has opened.
Lighting an empty space and lighting a space full of people moving
around is completely different. After he's happy with the setting,
he'll throw away the key to the box so no one can ever change it.

How much of this can you model, or is it more instinctive?

It's not something you can model on a computer. It's too subtle. If
you're designing a lighting scheme for an office you could paint a
picture, because it's all fluorescents, but in projects like Hakkasan
it's all about feeling. If you take six different types of halogen bulb,
each one will give you a slightly different feeling. One with a glass
reflector will give warmer light than one with a metal reflector. The
metal reflector gives a much tighter, sharper beam so I can accent
something like a glass of water much more effectively. But one with
a glass reflector does something else.

It's not something you can learn from books. It really is about
experience in the field. Which is why there aren't so many lighting
designers, although there are loads of architects and loads of
interior designers.

In lighting design, you need the technical discipline and you need
the theatrical or artistic discipline. But you also need to understand
the architecture, to be able to read the plan, and to be able to

perceive in three dimensions. How is this space going to be? How am I going to paint it with light? How is it going to merge with the detailing of materials? It's very difficult to study all of that in one go. So much of lighting is about subtle, minute little finesses, and a lot of it is subliminal in a way. People tend to notice bad lighting. When lighting works and is done well, they just feel that the space and the environment are good.

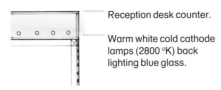

Reception desk counter.

Warm white cold cathode
lamps (2800 °K) back
lighting blue glass.

The reception area at
London's Hakkasan. The
restaurant is located in a
basement space. Detail
drawings (left) for lighting
design and colour rendering
of reception lighting (below).

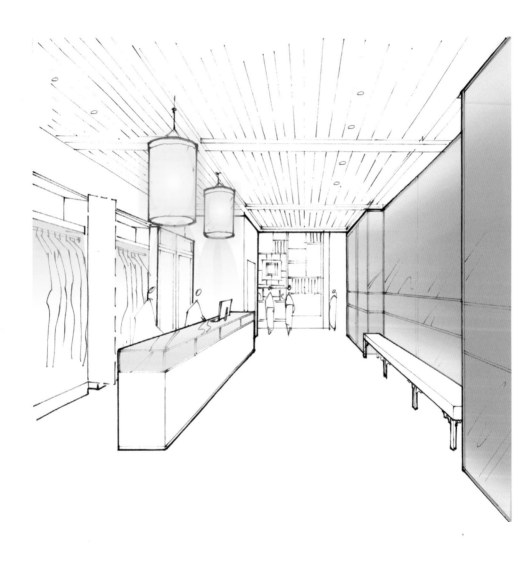

The long bar at Hakkasan
features a slate wall
evocatively lit by theatrical
projectors to create a rippling
effect, reminiscent of water.
The fittings had to be
adapted technically, and were
integrated into the design
so they were not obvious.

Overleaf: Long trough
lights illuminate the wine
serving area.

Surface-mounted Gobo
projector with spinning
effects wheel to create
ripple effect.

Heavily textured wall.

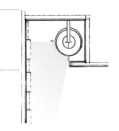

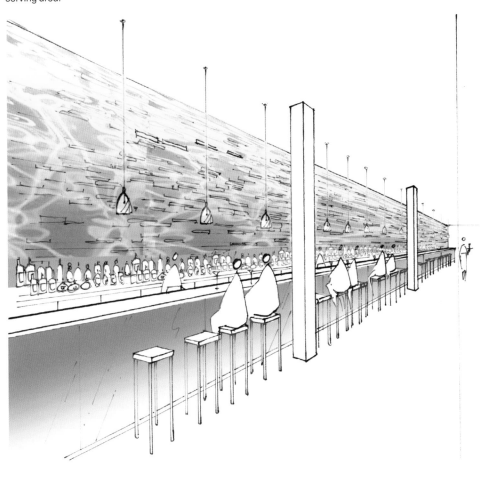

The main dining area at Hakkasan is dramatically lit to create a mysterious ambience. Raking light from narrow pencil-beam spots picks out details of the screens that subdivide the space. The blue wall is backlit with cold cathode sources at the top and bottom.

Overleaf: View of the bar through the screens.

Light is directed at the tabletops to provide a focus of intimacy and draw attention to the food.

Preceding pages: The pre-programmed light levels change subtly throughout the evening.

Selected works

Designer:
Arnold Chan

Buddakan, 2006

An old cookie factory in
Manhattan provides the
setting for this fusion
restaurant opened by Alan
Yau. Smooth backlighting
to the artwork panel blends
with the banquette wash
lighting to bring out the
warmth of the brickwork.

Buddakan

The walls of the great hall are lined with oak and a banquet table takes centre stage, lit by giant chandeliers. Expressed in a very theatrical manner, the high contrast textures of projected light emphasize the performance aspect of haute cuisine.

St Martin's Lane Hotel, 1999

For American hotelier Ian Shrager's first London hotel, Chan worked in collaboration with Philippe Starck, who was responsible for the interior design. Bare light bulbs hang over the restaurant tables, while in the lobby area subtle lighting accentuates the fluorescent yellow walls.

Gramercy Park Hotel, 2007

The private club at the Gramercy Park Hotel features a ceiling dramatically filled with used lamps, among which a small fraction are powered to create a warm glow within the filaments. The lighting concept was referenced from a Jeff Wall portrait.

Index

Figures in italics
indicate captions.

0024 hanging light 50, *50*
85 Lamps *63*
2097/50 hanging light 54, *54*
Akari series 17, *18*
ambient light *8*, 15, *17*
Anglepoise lamp 25, *25*
Arad, Ron *4*
architectural lighting 80
Arco floor lamp *56*, 59
Art Institute of Chicago *8*
Art Nouveau 45
Arteluce 53, 54
Artemide 54
Artichoke *32*

Baccarat 10, *13*
backlighting 28, *38*, 79, *92*, *101*
baffles *15*
bare light bulbs 17, 45, *45*, 80, *104*
bare-wire installations 64
Bauhaus 47, *48*
Berenice *15*
Bettonica, Franco 64, *64*
Bilia lamp 50, *50*
Boontje, Tord 18, *23*
Buddakan restaurant, 72, *101*, *102*

Calatrava, Santiago 31
Calder, Alexander 54
candlelight 38, 42, 45
candles 42, *42*, 47
candlesticks 45
Carwardine, George 25, *25*
Castiglioni, Achille *56*, *56*, 59, *59*
Castiglioni, Pier 53, 56, *56*
Castiglioni brothers 53, 56, 59
CFL (compact fluorescent lamp) *38*, 41, 110
Chan, Arnold (case study) 70–99
chandeliers *4*, *6*, 45, 47, *102*
Chiesa, Pietro 28, 53

Chimera light *53*, 54
Chipperfield, David 72, 74, 75
Chopstick light 64
Clothes Hanger lamp 59, *63*
cochin (paper lanterns) 17
Cocksedge, Paul 59, *60*, 67, *67*
'coiled coil' filament 80
cold cathode light 78, 79, *86*, *92*, 110
colour 38–41
    rendering 78, 79, *86*
    temperature 78, 81
concealed lighting 47
Constellation 32, *37*
Covent Garden Market, 32, *37*

Danish National Pavilion 20
daylight 38, 42
De Lucchi, Michele 25, *27*
diffusers 50, *60*, 83
diffusion 17-23
dimmer switches 46
dimming lights 15, 83
direction 24–7
Dixon, Tom 31, *31*
Domus magazine 50, 53
downlights *15*, 25
Droog Design *6*, 59, *63*

Echelle ('Ladder') *32*
Eden Project 67
Edison, Thomas 38, 45, 80
El.E Dee light 16, *16*
Eight-Fifty light 59, *60*
electric age, the 44–6
emotion 32–7
energy-efficient light sources 15–16, *38*

Fassina, Giancarlo 25, *27*
fibre optics 64, *64*, 67, 110
Field of Light 67
firelight 42, *42*
floor light 28, 31, 110
Flos 10, *13*, 53, 67
fluorescent light 38, *38*, 78, 84, *104*, 110
Fontana Arte 28, *50*, 53

Fontana table lamp 28, 31
Fortuny lamp 45
Fortuny y Madrazo, Mariano 45–6, *45*
Foscarini 53
function 14–16

Garland light 18, *23*
gaslight 45
General Electric 38
glare 17, 45, 83
Glo-ball *17*
Gobo projector *89*
Gramercy Park Hotel 72, 84, *106*
Graumans, Rody *63*
Gray, Eileen 48, 50, *50*

Haaa!!! floor lamp 10, *13*
Habitat 18, *23*, 60
Hadid, Zaha 72
Hakkasan restaurant 70–99
halogen light 31, *35*, 38, 41, *41*, 64, 78, 84, 110
Hammond, Robert *46*
Haselden, Ron *32*
Henningsen, Poul 18, *20*, 28
Herbert Terry & Sons 25, *25*
Hirst, Damian 72, 81
Holzer, Jenny 10, *13*
Hooo!!! table lamp 10

incandescent light 16, 38, 42, 45, 78, 110
Ingrand, Max 28, *31*
Isometrix Lighting + Design 72

Jack light 31, *31*
Jill light 28, 31
John Cullen Lighting *15*
Jucker, Karl J 47, *48*

King, Perry 31

La Roche, Raoul 48
Lacrime del Pescatore ('The Fisherman's Tears') *35*, 37
Laelia light *64*

Langelinie Pavilion 20
Lantern Parade 42
lanterns 17, 45
LCDs (liquid crystal displays) 110
Le Corbusier 47, 48
LEDs (light-emitting diodes) 4, 10, 16, 16, 32, 37, 41, 67, 78, 110
Leipzig Trade Fair (1924) 47
Liagre, Christian 72, 75–6, 79, 80
Life 01 67, 67
light-as-object 28, 31, 31
London Design Festival 67
Loop.ph 67, 69
low-efficiency light bulbs 67
low-energy lighting 67
Lucellino 35
Luceplan 53
Lumière festival of light 32
Luminator 28

Magistretti, Vico 53, 53, 54
Manzù, Pio 59, 59
Marston, Sharon 64, 64
Maugham, Syrie 47
Maurer, Ingo 16, 16, 23, 32, 35, 37, 37
Meda, Alberto 15
Melocchi, Mario 64, 64
Memphis style 53
Mezzandro stool 56
Milan Salone (2009) 10
Milk Bottle lamp 6, 59
Mira 50 15
Miranda, Santiago 31
Miss Sissi light 10, 10
Modernism 47–51, 110
Montjuic uplight 31
Moore, Daniel McFarlan 38
Morano glass 53
Morgan, John Pierpont 45
Morrison, Jasper 17
Munro, Bruce 67

natural light 6, 15, 48
neon 32

Noguchi, Isamu 17, 18
Norcross, Claire 59, 60
Nouvel, Jean 72

oil lamps 42

Panton, Verner 28
PAR (parabolic alluminized reflector) lamp 110
Parentesi 56, 59, 59
Pawson, John 72, 74, 75, 82
pendant lights 25, 28, 45, 79–80, 83, 110
PH Artichoke light 18, 20
PH series 18
Pharmacy restaurant 72, 81
Ponti, Giò 50, 50, 53
Porca Misèria 32, 37, 37
postmodernism 110
programming, electronic 15, 99
projected lighting 47, 102

raking light 81, 92
rationalism 53–4, 53
ready-mades 6, 56–63
reconstruction (ricostruzione) 53
reflection 8, 42
reflectors 48
refraction 110
Remy, Tejo 6, 59
Rizzatto, Paolo 15
Rogers, Richard 72
Romeo Moon 31
Roquebrune-Cap-Martin 50
rush lights 42

safety standards 15
St Martin's Lane Hotel 72, 80, 104
Salisbury Festival 32
Sapper, Richard 25, 27
Sarfatti, Gino 53, 54, 54
Schrager, Ian 72, 84, 104
Selfridges department store 72
Serrano, Héctor 59, 63
Shell lights 28
Sonumbra 67, 69

Sottsass, Ettore 53
spatial description 28–31
spotlights 6, 8, 25, 92
stage lighting 80
standard lamps 31
Starck, Philippe 10, 10, 13, 31, 72, 74, 80, 104
strip lights 38, 48
Styrene 59, 60
Swarovski 4
switching 15

table lights 28, 31, 110
task lighting 15, 25
Tenso system 64, 64
theatrical projectors 80, 89
Tiffany 45
Tizio task light 25, 27
Toio 56, 59, 60
Tolomeo light 25, 27
track lighting 64, 64
trough lights 89
Tube light 50, 50
tungsten 31, 38, 41, 110

uplights 25
UVA (United Visual Artists) 32, 37

Villa La Roche, Paris 48
voltage 110

Wagamama 75
Wagenfeld, Wilhelm 47, 48
Waldemeyer, Moritz 10, 13
Wall, Jeff 106
wallwashers 15, 25, 110
washi (mulberry bark paper) 17, 18
water, and safety standards 15
wattage 77, 110
Wednesday light 18, 23
WG24 47, 48
Williams, Tennessee 17

Yau, Alan 72, 75, 76, 78, 79, 101

Zettel'z 6 light 23

Glossary

CFL *Compact fluorescent lamp*, or energy-saving bulb – a development of the fluorescent light now widely adopted in domestic lighting.

cold cathode light A form of fluorescent lighting that is often used for long-life applications such as the backlights for liquid crystal displays (LCDs). Because cold cathode lights can also take the form of very long tubes or series of tubes, they are also often used to create commercial signage.

downlight A light fixture, usually set into a recess in a ceiling, that projects light downwards into a room.

fibre optics Glass or plastic fibres that, using the principle of refraction, are able to transmit light invisibly along their lengths. Fibre optics are widely used in communications technology and also in illuminations, where they are often deployed in bundles.

floor light A free-standing, vertical light, often shaded, and sometimes known as a standard lamp.

fluorescent light In this form of lighting, an electric current is passed through a tube containing mercury vapour, which then produces ultraviolet light. This in turn causes a phosphor (usually some kind of metal compound) to emit light –

to fluoresce. The fluorescent tube is more energy-efficient than incandescent lights but the flat, stark light it produces meant that, until the development of the CFL, its use was mostly confined to public buildings, where energy efficiency is key.

halogen light A form of incandescent light that features a tungsten filament and a bulb that encloses a small amount of halogen (often iodine or bromine). Such lights have a longer life than ordinary incandescent bulbs, and produce a whiter light that gives improved colour rendering.

incandescent light In this form of lighting, an electric current is passed through a fine filament enclosed in an evacuated glass bulb, thereby producing light but also a very high percentage of heat. The inefficiency of this electric lighting method and the development of the energy-saving bulb (or CFL) have led to incandescent light bulbs being phased out in many countries.

LED (light-emitting diode) A semiconductor light source, first used commercially from the 1960s for indicators in calculators, TVs, traffic signals and cars, etc., but today becoming more widely deployed in ordinary lighting.

PAR lamp *Parabolic aluminized reflector* – a lamp

that uses lens and reflectors to create a powerful beam of light. PARs are often used in stage lighting, locomotive headlamps, and in domestic or commercial settings as mood-setting downlights.

pendant light One of the main light types: designed to hang from the ceiling. Pendants are designed to provide the general illumination of a room and, as with the chandelier, can be a focal design feature.

spotlight A light designed to project an intense, narrow beam of light.

table light A common type of lighting usually comprising a base and a shade, and used to provide ambient lighting.

task light A usually adjustable light designed to illuminate a work area such as a desk or drawing board.

uplight A light fixture, usually on or close to the floor, that throws ambient light upwards across a wall or to a ceiling.

voltage The potential electric force – analogous, to a degree, with water pressure (SI unit = volt).

Wallwasher A light that illuminates a wall evenly without lighting the floor.

wattage The amount of electrical power (SI unit = watt).

Picture Credits

The publisher would like to thank the following photographers and agencies for their kind permission to reproduce the following photographs:

2 Ph: Spencer Tsai/Ron Arad Associates; 7 Chris Tubbs/ Red Cover; 8 Arch: Abeijon-Fernandez/Ph: Santos-Diez/ fabpics/Arcaid; 9 above Arch: Hun T.W. Hung/Ph: Marc Gerritsen/ Arcaid; 9 below Christian Richters/VIEW; 11 Philippe Starck; 12–13 Flos/Philippe Starck; 14 above John Cullen Lighting; 14 below Alberto Meda; 16 Ph: Tom Vack/ Ingo Maurer GmbH, Munich; 17 Flos; 19 above © The Isamu Noguchi Foundation and Garden Museum/ARS, New York and DACS, London; 19 below Ph: John Berens/ ©The Isamu Noguchi Foundation and Garden Museum/ARS, New York and DACS, London; 20–21 Louis Poulsen; 22 Studio Tord Boontje; 23 Ph: Tom Vack/Ingo Maurer GmbH, Munich; 24 Anglepoise Holdings Ltd; 26 Artemide; 27 Michele de Lucchi Archive; 28 Fontana Arte; 29 Verner Panton Design; 30 Flos/Philippe Starck; 31 www.rume.co.uk; 33 Matthew Andrews; 34–36 Ph: Tom Vack/Ingo Maurer GmbH Munich; 37 UVA/ James Medraft + Jane Stockdale; 38 David Young-Wolff/Alamy; 39 Filip Dujardin;

40 Jansje Klazinga/Taverne; 41 below left Dominique Faget/AFP/ Getty Images; 41 above left Linda Phillips/ Science Photo Library; 41 right Tom Scott/Red Cover; 43 below David Wall/Alamy; 43 above Ray Main/ Mainstreamimages /fewandfar.net; 45 Gelantin silver bromide print 18x24cm c1905. Archivio Fotografico Museo Fortuny/Fondazione Musei Civici di Venezia. 46 Science & Society Picture Library; 49 © 2010. Digital image. The Museum of Modern Art, New York/Scala, Florence; 50 ClassiCon GmbH; 51 Gio Ponti Archives; 52 Artemide; 55 Ed Reeve/ Red Cover; 56–58 Museo Achille Castiglioni/Triennale Design Museum/La Triennale di Milano; 60 Flos; 61 above Ph: Richard Brine/Paul Cocksedge Studio; 61 below Ph: Tim Ainsworth/Claire Norcross; 62–63 Ph: Gerard van Hees/Droog Design; 65 below Ph: Daniel Brooke/ Sharon Marston; 65 above Cini & Nil; 66 below Ph: Alex Wilson/Bruce Munro Ltd; 66 above Ph: Mark Pickthall/ Bruce Munro Ltd; 67 Flos/ Paul Cocksedge Studio; 68 Studio Loop.pH; 71 Moris Moreno; 86 Isometrix; 87–88 Moris Moreno; 89 Isometrix; 90 Moris Moreno; 92 Isometrix; 93–94 & 96-99 Moris Moreno; 101–102 David Joseph/Starr Restaurant Organisation; 104–105 Morgan Hotel Group; 106–107 Ian Schrager Company.

Every effort has been made to trace the copyright holders. We apologise in advance for any unintentional omissions and would be pleased to insert the appropriate acknowledgement in any subsequent publication.

Credits

First published in 2010
by Conran Octopus Ltd
in association with
The Design Museum

Conran Octopus,
a part of Octopus Publishing
Group, Endeavour House,
189 Shaftesbury Avenue,
London WC2H 8JY
www.octopusbooks.co.uk

A Hachette UK Company
www.hachette.co.uk

Distributed in the United
States and Canada by
Hachette Book Group USA,
237 Park Avenue, New York,
NY 10017 USA

British Library Cataloguing-
in-Publication Data.
A catalogue record for
this book is available
from the British Library.

Text written by:
Elizabeth Wilhide

Publisher:
Lorraine Dickey
Consultant Editor:
Deyan Sudjic
Managing Editor:
Sybella Marlow
Editor:
Robert Anderson

Art Director:
Jonathan Christie
Design:
Untitled
Picture Researcher:
Anne-Marie Hoines

Production Manager:
Katherine Hockley

ISBN: 978 1 84091 547 1
Printed in China